35 Salad Recipes for Home

By: Kelly Johnson

Table of Contents

Salads:

- Caesar Salad
- Greek Salad
- Caprese Salad
- Cobb Salad
- Waldorf Salad
- Spinach and Strawberry Salad
- Quinoa Salad
- Asian Noodle Salad
- Kale and Avocado Salad
- Mediterranean Chickpea Salad
- Watermelon Feta Salad
- Roasted Vegetable Salad
- Tuna Nicoise Salad
- Beet and Goat Cheese Salad
- Southwest Black Bean Salad
- Chicken Caesar Salad
- Mango Salsa Salad
- Shrimp and Avocado Salad
- Broccoli Salad
- Apple Pecan Salad
- Thai Peanut Noodle Salad
- Couscous Salad
- Mexican Street Corn Salad
- Potato Salad
- Roasted Brussels Sprouts Salad
- Italian Pasta Salad
- Tomato and Mozzarella Salad
- Cucumber Dill Salad
- Caesar Pasta Salad
- Chicken and Quinoa Salad
- Roasted Red Pepper and Artichoke Salad
- Spring Mix Salad with Raspberry Vinaigrette
- Edamame and Sesame Salad
- Caprese Pasta Salad
- Orange and Almond Salad

Caesar Salad

Ingredients:

- 1 head of romaine lettuce, washed and chopped
- 1 cup croutons (store-bought or homemade)
- 1/2 cup freshly grated Parmesan cheese
- Caesar dressing (homemade or store-bought)
- Freshly ground black pepper, to taste
- Lemon wedges, for serving

Caesar Dressing:

- 1/2 cup mayonnaise
- 1/4 cup grated Parmesan cheese
- 2 tablespoons Dijon mustard
- 2 cloves garlic, minced
- 1 tablespoon anchovy paste (optional, for a traditional Caesar flavor)
- 1 tablespoon Worcestershire sauce
- 2 tablespoons fresh lemon juice
- Salt and pepper, to taste

Instructions:

Prepare the Dressing:
- In a bowl, whisk together mayonnaise, Parmesan cheese, Dijon mustard, minced garlic, anchovy paste (if using), Worcestershire sauce, fresh lemon juice, salt, and pepper. Adjust seasoning to taste.

Assemble the Salad:
- In a large salad bowl, combine the chopped romaine lettuce and croutons.

Add Dressing:
- Add enough Caesar dressing to coat the lettuce and croutons. Toss the salad until everything is evenly coated with the dressing.

Top with Parmesan:
- Sprinkle freshly grated Parmesan cheese over the salad.

Serve:
- Divide the Caesar Salad onto individual plates. Grind black pepper over the top and garnish with additional Parmesan if desired.

Optional:

- You can add grilled chicken, shrimp, or bacon for added protein.

Serve with Lemon Wedges:
- Serve the Caesar Salad with lemon wedges on the side for squeezing over the salad before eating.

Enjoy your delicious homemade Caesar Salad!

Greek Salad

Ingredients:

For the Salad:

- 1 cucumber, diced
- 1 red bell pepper, diced
- 1 green bell pepper, diced
- 1 cup cherry tomatoes, halved
- 1 red onion, thinly sliced
- 1 cup Kalamata olives, pitted
- 1 cup crumbled feta cheese
- 1/2 cup fresh parsley, chopped
- Salt and pepper, to taste

For the Dressing:

- 1/3 cup extra virgin olive oil
- 3 tablespoons red wine vinegar
- 1 teaspoon dried oregano
- 1 teaspoon Dijon mustard
- 1 clove garlic, minced
- Salt and pepper, to taste

Instructions:

    Prepare the Vegetables:
- In a large salad bowl, combine the diced cucumber, red bell pepper, green bell pepper, cherry tomatoes, red onion, Kalamata olives, and crumbled feta cheese.

    Make the Dressing:
- In a small bowl, whisk together the olive oil, red wine vinegar, dried oregano, Dijon mustard, minced garlic, salt, and pepper.

    Dress the Salad:
- Pour the dressing over the salad ingredients.

    Toss and Season:
- Gently toss the salad to coat all the vegetables and feta with the dressing. Add salt and pepper to taste.

    Chill (Optional):

- If time allows, let the Greek Salad chill in the refrigerator for about 30 minutes to let the flavors meld.

Garnish:
- Sprinkle chopped fresh parsley over the top before serving.

Serve:
- Serve the Greek Salad on its own or as a side dish. It pairs well with grilled meats or can be enjoyed on its own.

This Greek Salad is refreshing, full of vibrant colors, and packed with Mediterranean flavors. Enjoy!

Caprese Salad

Ingredients:

- 4 large ripe tomatoes, sliced
- 1 pound fresh mozzarella cheese, sliced
- Fresh basil leaves
- Extra virgin olive oil
- Balsamic glaze (optional)
- Salt and black pepper, to taste

Instructions:

Slice Tomatoes and Mozzarella:
- Wash and slice the tomatoes and fresh mozzarella cheese into even, medium-thick slices.

Assemble the Salad:
- Arrange the tomato and mozzarella slices alternately on a serving platter, creating a visually appealing pattern.

Add Basil Leaves:
- Tuck fresh basil leaves between the tomato and mozzarella slices. You can leave the leaves whole or tear them into smaller pieces.

Drizzle with Olive Oil:
- Drizzle extra virgin olive oil over the salad. This adds a rich flavor to the dish.

Season with Salt and Pepper:
- Sprinkle salt and black pepper over the salad to taste. Remember that the mozzarella may already have some saltiness, so adjust accordingly.

Optional Balsamic Glaze:
- For an extra touch of sweetness and acidity, you can drizzle balsamic glaze over the salad. This step is optional but adds a delightful flavor.

Serve Fresh:
- Caprese Salad is best enjoyed fresh. Serve immediately to preserve the vibrant colors and flavors.

Variations:
- You can enhance the Caprese Salad by adding extras like pine nuts, olives, or a sprinkle of dried oregano.

This simple and elegant Caprese Salad is perfect as an appetizer, a light lunch, or a side dish for any Italian-inspired meal. Enjoy!

Cobb Salad

Ingredients:

For the Salad:

- 4 cups mixed salad greens (lettuce, arugula, or a blend)
- 2 cups cooked and diced chicken breast
- 1 cup cherry tomatoes, halved
- 1 avocado, diced
- 4 hard-boiled eggs, chopped
- 1 cup crumbled blue cheese or Roquefort cheese
- 6 slices bacon, cooked and crumbled
- Chopped green onions (optional, for garnish)

For the Dressing:

- 1/4 cup extra virgin olive oil
- 2 tablespoons red wine vinegar
- 1 teaspoon Dijon mustard
- 1 clove garlic, minced
- Salt and pepper, to taste

Instructions:

Prepare the Salad Greens:
- Arrange the mixed salad greens on a large serving platter or in a salad bowl.

Assemble the Salad:
- Arrange the cooked and diced chicken, cherry tomatoes, diced avocado, chopped hard-boiled eggs, crumbled blue cheese, and crumbled bacon in rows or sections on top of the salad greens.

Make the Dressing:
- In a small bowl, whisk together the olive oil, red wine vinegar, Dijon mustard, minced garlic, salt, and pepper until well combined.

Drizzle Dressing:
- Drizzle the dressing over the Cobb Salad. You can use as much or as little as you prefer.

Toss or Serve as is:

- If serving immediately, you can toss the salad gently to coat the ingredients with the dressing. Alternatively, serve it as is, allowing each person to mix their salad at the table.

Garnish:
- Garnish with chopped green onions if desired.

Serve:
- Serve the Cobb Salad immediately, and enjoy this flavorful and satisfying meal.

Cobb Salad is not only delicious but also versatile. Feel free to customize it with your favorite salad ingredients or adjust the dressing to suit your taste.

Waldorf Salad

Ingredients:

For the Salad:

- 2 cups diced apples (use a combination of sweet and tart apples)
- 1 cup diced celery
- 1 cup red seedless grapes, halved
- 1 cup chopped walnuts
- 1/2 cup raisins (optional)

For the Dressing:

- 1/2 cup mayonnaise
- 1/4 cup plain Greek yogurt
- 1 tablespoon honey
- 1 tablespoon fresh lemon juice
- Salt and pepper, to taste

For Garnish:

- Fresh parsley leaves (optional)

Instructions:

Prepare Ingredients:
- Wash, peel (if desired), and dice the apples. Dice the celery, halve the grapes, and chop the walnuts.

Make the Dressing:
- In a small bowl, whisk together mayonnaise, Greek yogurt, honey, fresh lemon juice, salt, and pepper until well combined. Adjust sweetness and acidity to taste.

Combine Salad Ingredients:
- In a large mixing bowl, combine the diced apples, diced celery, halved grapes, chopped walnuts, and raisins (if using).

Add Dressing:
- Pour the dressing over the salad ingredients and gently toss until everything is evenly coated.

Chill (Optional):

- For enhanced flavors, you can refrigerate the Waldorf Salad for about 30 minutes before serving.

Garnish:
- Garnish with fresh parsley leaves for a touch of color and added freshness.

Serve:
- Serve the Waldorf Salad as a side dish or a light meal. It's a refreshing and satisfying salad with a delightful combination of textures and flavors.

Feel free to customize this Waldorf Salad by adjusting the ingredient quantities or adding other ingredients like shredded chicken or chopped celery leaves. Enjoy this classic dish!

Spinach and Strawberry Salad

Ingredients:

For the Salad:

- 6 cups fresh baby spinach leaves, washed and dried
- 2 cups fresh strawberries, hulled and sliced
- 1/2 cup sliced almonds, toasted
- 1/4 cup crumbled feta cheese (optional)

For the Dressing:

- 3 tablespoons balsamic vinegar
- 2 tablespoons extra virgin olive oil
- 1 tablespoon honey
- 1 teaspoon Dijon mustard
- Salt and pepper, to taste

Instructions:

Prepare the Salad Ingredients:
- In a large salad bowl, combine the fresh baby spinach leaves, sliced strawberries, toasted sliced almonds, and crumbled feta cheese (if using).

Make the Dressing:
- In a small bowl, whisk together balsamic vinegar, extra virgin olive oil, honey, Dijon mustard, salt, and pepper until well combined.

Dress the Salad:
- Drizzle the dressing over the salad ingredients.

Toss Gently:
- Gently toss the salad until the dressing evenly coats the spinach, strawberries, and other ingredients.

Serve:
- Transfer the Spinach and Strawberry Salad to individual serving plates or bowls.

Optional Additions:
- If desired, you can add grilled chicken or crumbled bacon for extra protein.

Garnish (Optional):
- Garnish with additional sliced strawberries or a sprinkle of toasted almonds for a decorative touch.

Serve Immediately:

- This salad is best enjoyed immediately after dressing to maintain the crispness of the spinach leaves.

This Spinach and Strawberry Salad is not only visually appealing but also a delightful blend of sweet and savory flavors. It's perfect for a light lunch, as a side dish, or for a refreshing addition to a summer meal. Enjoy!

Quinoa Salad

Ingredients:

For the Salad:

- 1 cup quinoa, rinsed and cooked according to package instructions
- 1 cucumber, diced
- 1 red bell pepper, diced
- 1 cup cherry tomatoes, halved
- 1/2 cup red onion, finely chopped
- 1/2 cup feta cheese, crumbled
- 1/4 cup Kalamata olives, pitted and sliced
- Fresh parsley, chopped (for garnish)

For the Dressing:

- 1/4 cup extra virgin olive oil
- 2 tablespoons red wine vinegar
- 1 teaspoon Dijon mustard
- 1 clove garlic, minced
- Salt and pepper, to taste

Instructions:

Prepare Quinoa:
- Rinse the quinoa under cold water. Cook the quinoa according to the package instructions. Once cooked, let it cool to room temperature.

Make the Dressing:
- In a small bowl, whisk together the olive oil, red wine vinegar, Dijon mustard, minced garlic, salt, and pepper. Set aside.

Assemble the Salad:
- In a large bowl, combine the cooked quinoa, diced cucumber, diced red bell pepper, cherry tomatoes, chopped red onion, crumbled feta cheese, and sliced Kalamata olives.

Add Dressing:
- Pour the dressing over the salad ingredients.

Toss Gently:
- Gently toss the salad until all ingredients are well coated with the dressing.

Chill (Optional):

- If time allows, refrigerate the Quinoa Salad for about 30 minutes to let the flavors meld.

Garnish:
- Garnish with freshly chopped parsley just before serving.

Serve:
- Serve the Quinoa Salad as a light and nutritious meal on its own or as a side dish. It's perfect for picnics, barbecues, or as a healthy lunch option.

Feel free to customize this Quinoa Salad by adding your favorite vegetables, nuts, or herbs. It's a versatile dish that can be adapted to suit your preferences. Enjoy!

Asian Noodle Salad

Ingredients:

For the Salad:

- 8 oz (about 225g) Asian noodles (such as soba, rice noodles, or udon), cooked and cooled
- 1 cup shredded cabbage
- 1 cup julienned carrots
- 1 red bell pepper, thinly sliced
- 1 cucumber, julienned
- 1/2 cup edamame, cooked and shelled
- 3 green onions, thinly sliced
- Sesame seeds and chopped cilantro for garnish

For the Dressing:

- 1/4 cup soy sauce
- 2 tablespoons sesame oil
- 2 tablespoons rice vinegar
- 1 tablespoon honey
- 1 tablespoon fresh ginger, grated
- 1 clove garlic, minced
- 1 tablespoon sesame seeds

Instructions:

Cook Noodles:
- Cook the Asian noodles according to the package instructions. Once cooked, rinse them under cold water to stop the cooking process and cool them down.

Prepare Vegetables:
- In a large mixing bowl, combine shredded cabbage, julienned carrots, sliced red bell pepper, julienned cucumber, edamame, and sliced green onions.

Combine Noodles and Vegetables:
- Add the cooled noodles to the bowl with vegetables.

Make the Dressing:

- In a small bowl, whisk together soy sauce, sesame oil, rice vinegar, honey, grated fresh ginger, minced garlic, and sesame seeds.

Toss Salad:
- Pour the dressing over the noodles and vegetables. Toss everything together until well coated.

Chill (Optional):
- If you have time, refrigerate the Asian Noodle Salad for about 30 minutes to allow the flavors to meld.

Garnish:
- Garnish the salad with sesame seeds and chopped cilantro.

Serve:
- Serve the Asian Noodle Salad as a refreshing and satisfying main dish or as a side dish for grilled proteins.

Feel free to customize this recipe by adding other ingredients such as sliced mushrooms, bell peppers, or protein like grilled chicken, shrimp, or tofu. Enjoy your Asian Noodle Salad!

Kale and Avocado Salad

Ingredients:

For the Salad:

- 1 bunch of kale, stems removed and leaves chopped
- 1 ripe avocado, diced
- 1 cup cherry tomatoes, halved
- 1/4 cup red onion, thinly sliced
- 1/4 cup feta cheese, crumbled (optional)
- 1/4 cup toasted pine nuts or almonds
- Lemon wedges for serving

For the Dressing:

- 3 tablespoons extra virgin olive oil
- 1 tablespoon balsamic vinegar
- 1 teaspoon Dijon mustard
- 1 clove garlic, minced
- Salt and pepper, to taste

Instructions:

Prepare Kale:
- Remove the stems from the kale leaves and chop the leaves into bite-sized pieces. Wash and pat dry.

Massage Kale:
- Place the chopped kale in a large bowl. Drizzle with a little olive oil and massage the kale with your hands for a few minutes to soften it.

Assemble Salad:
- Add diced avocado, halved cherry tomatoes, thinly sliced red onion, crumbled feta cheese (if using), and toasted pine nuts or almonds to the bowl with kale.

Make the Dressing:
- In a small bowl, whisk together extra virgin olive oil, balsamic vinegar, Dijon mustard, minced garlic, salt, and pepper until well combined.

Dress the Salad:
- Pour the dressing over the salad ingredients.

Toss Gently:

- Gently toss the salad until all ingredients are well coated with the dressing.

Chill (Optional):
- If time allows, refrigerate the Kale and Avocado Salad for about 15-30 minutes to let the flavors meld.

Serve:
- Serve the salad on individual plates or in a large bowl. Squeeze fresh lemon wedges over the salad just before serving.

This Kale and Avocado Salad is a nutritious and flavorful option, and the massaging technique helps to soften the kale leaves and improve the texture. Enjoy!

Mediterranean Chickpea Salad

Ingredients:

For the Salad:

- 2 cans (15 ounces each) chickpeas, drained and rinsed
- 1 cucumber, diced
- 1 cup cherry tomatoes, halved
- 1/2 red onion, finely chopped
- 1/2 cup Kalamata olives, pitted and sliced
- 1/2 cup crumbled feta cheese
- 1/4 cup fresh parsley, chopped
- 1/4 cup fresh mint, chopped

For the Dressing:

- 1/4 cup extra virgin olive oil
- 2 tablespoons red wine vinegar
- 1 teaspoon Dijon mustard
- 1 clove garlic, minced
- 1 teaspoon dried oregano
- Salt and pepper, to taste

Instructions:

Prepare Chickpeas:
- Drain and rinse the chickpeas thoroughly.

Make the Dressing:
- In a small bowl, whisk together the extra virgin olive oil, red wine vinegar, Dijon mustard, minced garlic, dried oregano, salt, and pepper.

Assemble Salad:
- In a large salad bowl, combine the chickpeas, diced cucumber, halved cherry tomatoes, finely chopped red onion, sliced Kalamata olives, crumbled feta cheese, chopped fresh parsley, and chopped fresh mint.

Add Dressing:
- Pour the dressing over the salad ingredients.

Toss Gently:
- Gently toss the salad until everything is well coated with the dressing.

Chill (Optional):

- If time allows, refrigerate the Mediterranean Chickpea Salad for about 30 minutes to let the flavors meld.

Serve:
- Serve the salad on a platter or individual plates. It can be enjoyed on its own or as a side dish.

Garnish (Optional):
- Garnish with additional fresh herbs or a drizzle of extra virgin olive oil before serving.

This Mediterranean Chickpea Salad is not only delicious but also full of vibrant colors and textures. It makes for a satisfying and healthy meal, perfect for lunch or as a side dish for a Mediterranean-inspired dinner. Enjoy!

Watermelon Feta Salad

Ingredients:

For the Salad:

- 4 cups cubed seedless watermelon
- 1 cup crumbled feta cheese
- 1/4 cup fresh mint leaves, chopped
- 1/4 cup red onion, thinly sliced
- 1 tablespoon extra virgin olive oil
- 1 tablespoon balsamic glaze (optional)
- Black pepper, to taste

Instructions:

Prepare Watermelon:
- Cut the watermelon into bite-sized cubes, removing seeds if any.

Assemble Salad:
- In a large salad bowl, combine the cubed watermelon, crumbled feta cheese, chopped fresh mint leaves, and thinly sliced red onion.

Drizzle with Olive Oil:
- Drizzle extra virgin olive oil over the salad. This adds a rich flavor to the dish.

Toss Gently:
- Gently toss the salad to combine all the ingredients.

Optional Balsamic Glaze:
- If desired, drizzle balsamic glaze over the Watermelon Feta Salad. This step is optional but adds a delightful sweetness.

Season with Black Pepper:
- Sprinkle black pepper over the salad to taste.

Chill (Optional):
- If time allows, refrigerate the salad for about 15-30 minutes to enhance the flavors.

Serve:
- Serve the Watermelon Feta Salad in a large bowl or individual plates. It's a refreshing and light dish, perfect for summer.

This salad is a great combination of sweet and savory flavors, making it a hit at picnics, barbecues, or as a side dish for various meals. Enjoy!

Roasted Vegetable Salad

Ingredients:

For the Roasted Vegetables:

- 2 cups cherry tomatoes, halved
- 2 bell peppers, diced (mix of colors)
- 1 zucchini, sliced
- 1 yellow squash, sliced
- 1 red onion, sliced
- 2 carrots, peeled and sliced
- 2 tablespoons olive oil
- 1 teaspoon dried thyme
- 1 teaspoon dried rosemary
- Salt and black pepper, to taste

For the Salad:

- Mixed salad greens (lettuce, arugula, spinach)
- 1/2 cup crumbled feta cheese
- Balsamic vinaigrette dressing

Instructions:

Preheat the Oven:
- Preheat your oven to 425°F (220°C).

Prepare Vegetables:
- In a large mixing bowl, combine the halved cherry tomatoes, diced bell peppers, sliced zucchini, sliced yellow squash, sliced red onion, and sliced carrots.

Toss with Olive Oil and Seasonings:
- Drizzle the vegetables with olive oil, dried thyme, dried rosemary, salt, and black pepper. Toss until the vegetables are evenly coated.

Roast Vegetables:
- Spread the vegetables in a single layer on a baking sheet. Roast in the preheated oven for about 20-25 minutes or until the vegetables are tender and slightly caramelized, stirring halfway through.

Assemble the Salad:
- In a large salad bowl, arrange a bed of mixed salad greens.

Add Roasted Vegetables:

- Once the roasted vegetables are done, allow them to cool for a few minutes. Add the warm or room temperature roasted vegetables on top of the mixed greens.

Sprinkle Feta Cheese:
- Sprinkle crumbled feta cheese over the roasted vegetables.

Drizzle with Dressing:
- Drizzle balsamic vinaigrette dressing over the salad according to your taste.

Toss Gently:
- Gently toss the salad to combine all the ingredients.

Serve:
- Serve the Roasted Vegetable Salad as a delicious and nutritious main dish or as a side dish with your favorite protein.

Feel free to customize the vegetables and seasonings based on your preferences. This salad is a versatile and hearty option that can be enjoyed warm or at room temperature. Enjoy!

Tuna Nicoise Salad

Ingredients:

For the Salad:

- 2 cups baby potatoes, halved or quartered
- 1 cup green beans, trimmed
- 1 cup cherry tomatoes, halved
- 1/2 cup Nicoise olives (or Kalamata olives)
- 4 hard-boiled eggs, halved
- 1 can (6-7 ounces) tuna, drained (preferably packed in olive oil)
- Mixed salad greens (lettuce, arugula, or spinach)

For the Dressing:

- 3 tablespoons extra virgin olive oil
- 1 tablespoon red wine vinegar
- 1 teaspoon Dijon mustard
- 1 clove garlic, minced
- Salt and black pepper, to taste

Instructions:

Cook Potatoes:
- Boil or steam the baby potatoes until they are tender. Once cooked, let them cool to room temperature.

Blanch Green Beans:
- Blanch the green beans in boiling water for about 3 minutes or until they are crisp-tender. Transfer them to ice water to stop the cooking process and retain their vibrant color.

Prepare Tuna:
- If using canned tuna in oil, drain the oil. If using tuna in water, you may want to drizzle a little olive oil over the tuna for added flavor.

Assemble Salad:
- On a large serving platter or individual plates, arrange the mixed salad greens. Add the halved baby potatoes, blanched green beans, cherry tomatoes, Nicoise olives, hard-boiled eggs, and flaked tuna on top of the greens.

Make the Dressing:

- In a small bowl, whisk together extra virgin olive oil, red wine vinegar, Dijon mustard, minced garlic, salt, and black pepper until well combined.

Drizzle Dressing:
- Drizzle the dressing over the Tuna Nicoise Salad.

Serve:
- Serve the salad immediately, allowing each person to mix the salad at the table.

This Tuna Nicoise Salad is not only visually appealing but also a balanced and satisfying meal. It's perfect for a light lunch or dinner, especially in warmer weather. Enjoy!

Beet and Goat Cheese Salad

Ingredients:

For the Salad:

- 4 medium-sized beets, cooked and peeled, sliced into rounds or cubes
- 4 cups mixed salad greens (arugula, spinach, or mixed greens)
- 1/2 cup crumbled goat cheese
- 1/4 cup walnuts or candied pecans, chopped
- 1/4 cup red onion, thinly sliced
- Microgreens or fresh herbs for garnish (optional)

For the Dressing:

- 3 tablespoons extra virgin olive oil
- 2 tablespoons balsamic vinegar
- 1 tablespoon honey
- Salt and black pepper, to taste

Instructions:

Prepare Beets:
- Cook the beets by roasting or boiling until tender. Once cooled, peel the beets and slice them into rounds or cubes.

Assemble the Salad:
- On a large serving platter or individual plates, arrange the mixed salad greens. Top with the sliced beets, crumbled goat cheese, chopped walnuts or candied pecans, and thinly sliced red onion.

Make the Dressing:
- In a small bowl, whisk together extra virgin olive oil, balsamic vinegar, honey, salt, and black pepper until well combined.

Drizzle Dressing:
- Drizzle the dressing over the Beet and Goat Cheese Salad.

Garnish:
- Garnish the salad with microgreens or fresh herbs for an extra burst of flavor and color.

Serve:
- Serve the salad immediately, or refrigerate for a short time before serving if you prefer it chilled.

This Beet and Goat Cheese Salad is a beautiful and flavorful option, perfect for a light lunch, a side dish, or a colorful addition to a festive meal. Enjoy!

Southwest Black Bean Salad

Ingredients:

For the Salad:

- 2 cans (15 ounces each) black beans, drained and rinsed
- 1 cup corn kernels (fresh, frozen, or canned)
- 1 red bell pepper, diced
- 1 orange or yellow bell pepper, diced
- 1 cup cherry tomatoes, halved
- 1/2 red onion, finely chopped
- 1 avocado, diced
- 1/4 cup fresh cilantro, chopped

For the Dressing:

- 3 tablespoons lime juice (about 2 limes)
- 3 tablespoons extra virgin olive oil
- 1 teaspoon ground cumin
- 1 teaspoon chili powder
- 1 clove garlic, minced
- Salt and black pepper, to taste

Instructions:

Prepare Black Beans:
- Drain and rinse the black beans under cold water. Allow them to drain thoroughly.

Assemble the Salad:
- In a large salad bowl, combine the black beans, corn kernels, diced red bell pepper, diced orange or yellow bell pepper, halved cherry tomatoes, finely chopped red onion, diced avocado, and chopped cilantro.

Make the Dressing:
- In a small bowl, whisk together lime juice, extra virgin olive oil, ground cumin, chili powder, minced garlic, salt, and black pepper until well combined.

Drizzle Dressing:
- Drizzle the dressing over the Southwest Black Bean Salad.

Toss Gently:

- Gently toss the salad to ensure all the ingredients are well coated with the dressing.

Chill (Optional):
- Refrigerate the salad for about 30 minutes to allow the flavors to meld, or serve it immediately.

Serve:
- Serve the Southwest Black Bean Salad as a side dish, a topping for tacos, or as a light and nutritious meal on its own.

Feel free to customize this salad by adding ingredients like diced jalapeños, shredded cheese, or a squeeze of additional lime juice for extra freshness. Enjoy your Southwest Black Bean Salad!

Chicken Caesar Salad

Ingredients:

For the Salad:

- 2 boneless, skinless chicken breasts
- Salt and black pepper, to taste
- 1 tablespoon olive oil
- 1 large head of romaine lettuce, washed and chopped
- 1 cup cherry tomatoes, halved
- 1/2 cup croutons
- 1/4 cup grated Parmesan cheese

For the Caesar Dressing:

- 1/2 cup mayonnaise
- 2 tablespoons grated Parmesan cheese
- 2 tablespoons freshly squeezed lemon juice
- 1 tablespoon Dijon mustard
- 2 cloves garlic, minced
- 1 teaspoon Worcestershire sauce
- Salt and black pepper, to taste

Instructions:

Grill Chicken:
- Season the chicken breasts with salt and black pepper. Heat olive oil in a grill pan or skillet over medium-high heat. Grill the chicken for 5-7 minutes per side or until cooked through. Allow it to rest for a few minutes before slicing.

Prepare Caesar Dressing:
- In a small bowl, whisk together mayonnaise, grated Parmesan cheese, lemon juice, Dijon mustard, minced garlic, Worcestershire sauce, salt, and black pepper. Adjust the seasonings to taste.

Assemble the Salad:
- In a large salad bowl, combine the chopped romaine lettuce, cherry tomatoes, croutons, and sliced grilled chicken.

Add Caesar Dressing:
- Pour the Caesar dressing over the salad.

Toss Gently:

- Gently toss the salad to coat all ingredients with the dressing.

Top with Parmesan:
- Sprinkle grated Parmesan cheese over the salad.

Serve:
- Serve the Chicken Caesar Salad on individual plates. Optionally, garnish with additional croutons or extra Parmesan cheese.

Optional Additions:
- Feel free to customize your Chicken Caesar Salad by adding anchovies, bacon bits, or avocado.

This Chicken Caesar Salad is a delicious and satisfying meal, perfect for lunch or dinner. Enjoy the classic flavors!

Mango Salsa Salad

Ingredients:

For the Salad:

- 2 ripe mangoes, peeled, pitted, and diced
- 1 cup cherry tomatoes, halved
- 1 cucumber, diced
- 1/2 red bell pepper, diced
- 1/4 cup red onion, finely chopped
- 1 jalapeño, seeded and minced (optional for heat)
- 1/4 cup fresh cilantro, chopped
- 1 avocado, diced
- Mixed salad greens (lettuce, arugula, or spinach)

For the Dressing:

- 3 tablespoons lime juice (about 2 limes)
- 2 tablespoons extra virgin olive oil
- 1 teaspoon honey or agave nectar
- Salt and black pepper, to taste

Instructions:

Prepare Mangoes:
- Peel, pit, and dice the ripe mangoes.

Assemble the Salad:
- In a large salad bowl, combine the diced mangoes, halved cherry tomatoes, diced cucumber, diced red bell pepper, finely chopped red onion, minced jalapeño (if using), chopped cilantro, and diced avocado.

Make the Dressing:
- In a small bowl, whisk together lime juice, extra virgin olive oil, honey or agave nectar, salt, and black pepper until well combined.

Drizzle Dressing:
- Drizzle the dressing over the Mango Salsa Salad ingredients.

Toss Gently:
- Gently toss the salad to ensure all the ingredients are well coated with the dressing.

Chill (Optional):

- Refrigerate the salad for about 15-30 minutes to allow the flavors to meld, or serve it immediately.

Serve:
- Serve the Mango Salsa Salad on a bed of mixed salad greens.

Garnish (Optional):
- Garnish with additional cilantro or a sprinkle of black sesame seeds for a decorative touch.

This Mango Salsa Salad is a light and vibrant dish, perfect for a refreshing side salad or a light meal on its own. Enjoy the tropical flavors!

Shrimp and Avocado Salad

Ingredients:

For the Salad:

- 1 pound large shrimp, peeled and deveined
- 2 avocados, diced
- 1 cup cherry tomatoes, halved
- 1 cucumber, diced
- 1/4 cup red onion, finely chopped
- 1/4 cup fresh cilantro, chopped
- Mixed salad greens (lettuce, arugula, or spinach)

For the Dressing:

- 3 tablespoons lime juice (about 2 limes)
- 2 tablespoons extra virgin olive oil
- 1 clove garlic, minced
- 1 teaspoon honey or agave nectar
- Salt and black pepper, to taste

Instructions:

Cook Shrimp:
- In a large skillet over medium heat, cook the shrimp for 2-3 minutes per side or until they turn pink and opaque. Set aside to cool.

Prepare Vegetables:
- In a large salad bowl, combine diced avocados, halved cherry tomatoes, diced cucumber, finely chopped red onion, and chopped cilantro.

Assemble the Salad:
- Add the cooked shrimp to the bowl with the vegetables.

Make the Dressing:
- In a small bowl, whisk together lime juice, extra virgin olive oil, minced garlic, honey or agave nectar, salt, and black pepper.

Drizzle Dressing:
- Drizzle the dressing over the Shrimp and Avocado Salad.

Toss Gently:
- Gently toss the salad to coat all ingredients with the dressing.

Chill (Optional):

- Refrigerate the salad for about 15-30 minutes to let the flavors meld, or serve it immediately.

Serve:
- Serve the Shrimp and Avocado Salad on a bed of mixed salad greens.

Garnish (Optional):
- Garnish with additional cilantro or a wedge of lime for presentation.

This Shrimp and Avocado Salad is a refreshing and satisfying option, perfect for a light lunch or dinner. Enjoy the combination of succulent shrimp and creamy avocado!

Broccoli Salad

Ingredients:

For the Salad:

- 4 cups fresh broccoli florets, chopped into bite-sized pieces
- 1/2 cup red onion, finely chopped
- 1/2 cup raisins or dried cranberries
- 1/2 cup sunflower seeds or sliced almonds
- 1/2 cup shredded cheddar cheese (optional)

For the Dressing:

- 1 cup mayonnaise
- 1/4 cup sugar (adjust to taste)
- 2 tablespoons apple cider vinegar
- 1/2 teaspoon Dijon mustard
- Salt and black pepper, to taste

Instructions:

Prepare Broccoli:
- Wash and chop the fresh broccoli into bite-sized florets.

Assemble the Salad:
- In a large salad bowl, combine the chopped broccoli, finely chopped red onion, raisins or dried cranberries, sunflower seeds or sliced almonds, and shredded cheddar cheese (if using).

Make the Dressing:
- In a separate bowl, whisk together mayonnaise, sugar, apple cider vinegar, Dijon mustard, salt, and black pepper until the sugar is dissolved.

Combine Salad and Dressing:
- Pour the dressing over the broccoli mixture.

Toss Gently:
- Gently toss the salad until all ingredients are well coated with the dressing.

Chill (Optional):
- Refrigerate the Broccoli Salad for about 1-2 hours before serving to allow the flavors to meld.

Serve:

- Serve the Broccoli Salad as a side dish for picnics, barbecues, or as a refreshing addition to your meals.

This Broccoli Salad is not only delicious but also a great way to enjoy the crisp texture of broccoli with a sweet and tangy dressing. Feel free to customize the salad by adding other ingredients like bacon bits or chopped nuts. Enjoy!

Apple Pecan Salad

Ingredients:

For the Salad:

- 4 cups mixed salad greens (lettuce, arugula, or spinach)
- 2 apples, cored and thinly sliced (use your favorite variety)
- 1 cup pecans, toasted and chopped
- 1/2 cup crumbled blue cheese or feta cheese
- 1/4 cup red onion, thinly sliced

For the Dressing:

- 3 tablespoons apple cider vinegar
- 2 tablespoons extra virgin olive oil
- 1 tablespoon Dijon mustard
- 1 tablespoon honey
- Salt and black pepper, to taste

Instructions:

Prepare Salad Greens:
- Wash and dry the mixed salad greens. Place them in a large salad bowl.

Toast Pecans:
- In a dry skillet over medium heat, toast the pecans until fragrant and slightly browned. Allow them to cool, then chop coarsely.

Assemble the Salad:
- Arrange the thinly sliced apples, chopped pecans, crumbled blue cheese or feta, and thinly sliced red onion over the salad greens.

Make the Dressing:
- In a small bowl, whisk together apple cider vinegar, extra virgin olive oil, Dijon mustard, honey, salt, and black pepper until well combined.

Drizzle Dressing:
- Drizzle the dressing over the Apple Pecan Salad.

Toss Gently:
- Gently toss the salad until all ingredients are well coated with the dressing.

Serve:
- Serve the salad immediately, as the crispness of the apples and pecans is best enjoyed right away.

Optional Additions:
- If you like, you can add grilled chicken or thinly sliced turkey for extra protein.

This Apple Pecan Salad is a perfect blend of flavors and textures, making it a great choice for a light lunch or as a refreshing side dish for dinner. Enjoy!

Thai Peanut Noodle Salad

Ingredients:

For the Salad:

- 8 oz (about 225g) rice noodles or linguine, cooked and cooled
- 1 cup shredded carrots
- 1 cup red bell pepper, thinly sliced
- 1 cup cucumber, julienned
- 1/2 cup red cabbage, thinly sliced
- 1/4 cup green onions, sliced
- 1/4 cup fresh cilantro, chopped
- 1/4 cup peanuts, chopped (for garnish)

For the Peanut Sauce:

- 1/4 cup creamy peanut butter
- 2 tablespoons soy sauce
- 2 tablespoons rice vinegar
- 1 tablespoon sesame oil
- 1 tablespoon honey or maple syrup
- 1 clove garlic, minced
- 1 teaspoon fresh ginger, grated
- Red pepper flakes (optional, for heat)
- Water (as needed to thin the sauce)

Instructions:

Cook Noodles:
- Cook the rice noodles or linguine according to the package instructions. Once cooked, rinse them under cold water to stop the cooking process and cool them down.

Prepare Vegetables:
- In a large bowl, combine shredded carrots, thinly sliced red bell pepper, julienned cucumber, thinly sliced red cabbage, sliced green onions, and chopped cilantro.

Make Peanut Sauce:
- In a small bowl, whisk together peanut butter, soy sauce, rice vinegar, sesame oil, honey or maple syrup, minced garlic, grated ginger, and red

pepper flakes (if using). If the sauce is too thick, add water gradually to reach the desired consistency.

Combine Noodles and Vegetables:
- Add the cooled noodles to the bowl with vegetables.

Pour Peanut Sauce:
- Pour the peanut sauce over the noodles and vegetables.

Toss Gently:
- Gently toss the Thai Peanut Noodle Salad until everything is well coated with the peanut sauce.

Chill (Optional):
- Refrigerate the salad for about 30 minutes to let the flavors meld, or serve it immediately.

Garnish:
- Garnish the salad with chopped peanuts just before serving.

Serve:
- Serve the Thai Peanut Noodle Salad as a refreshing and flavorful main dish or as a side dish for grilled proteins.

This Thai Peanut Noodle Salad is a crowd-pleaser with its vibrant colors and bold flavors. Enjoy!

Couscous Salad

Ingredients:

For the Couscous:

- 1 cup couscous
- 1 cup boiling water or vegetable broth
- 1 tablespoon olive oil
- Salt, to taste

For the Salad:

- 1 cucumber, diced
- 1 bell pepper (any color), diced
- 1 cup cherry tomatoes, halved
- 1/4 cup red onion, finely chopped
- 1/4 cup Kalamata olives, sliced
- 1/4 cup feta cheese, crumbled
- Fresh herbs (parsley, mint, or cilantro), chopped

For the Dressing:

- 3 tablespoons extra virgin olive oil
- 2 tablespoons lemon juice
- 1 clove garlic, minced
- Salt and black pepper, to taste

Instructions:

Prepare Couscous:
- Place couscous in a heatproof bowl. Pour boiling water or vegetable broth over the couscous, add olive oil, and a pinch of salt. Cover the bowl with a lid or plastic wrap and let it sit for 5 minutes. Fluff the couscous with a fork to separate the grains.

Assemble the Salad:
- In a large salad bowl, combine the cooked and fluffed couscous with diced cucumber, diced bell pepper, halved cherry tomatoes, finely chopped red onion, sliced Kalamata olives, crumbled feta cheese, and chopped fresh herbs.

Make the Dressing:

- In a small bowl, whisk together extra virgin olive oil, lemon juice, minced garlic, salt, and black pepper.

Drizzle Dressing:
- Drizzle the dressing over the couscous and vegetable mixture.

Toss Gently:
- Gently toss the Couscous Salad until all ingredients are well coated with the dressing.

Chill (Optional):
- Refrigerate the salad for about 15-30 minutes to allow the flavors to meld, or serve it immediately.

Serve:
- Serve the Couscous Salad on its own as a light meal or as a side dish for grilled chicken, fish, or other proteins.

Feel free to customize this Couscous Salad by adding your favorite vegetables, nuts, or proteins.

It's a versatile and satisfying option for a quick and healthy meal. Enjoy!

Mexican Street Corn Salad

Ingredients:

For the Salad:

- 4 cups corn kernels (fresh, frozen, or canned)
- 1/2 cup mayonnaise
- 1/2 cup sour cream
- 1 cup cotija cheese, crumbled (substitute with feta or Parmesan if unavailable)
- 1/4 cup fresh cilantro, chopped
- 1/2 teaspoon chili powder (adjust to taste)
- 1 clove garlic, minced
- 1 jalapeño, finely chopped (optional for heat)
- Lime wedges, for serving

Instructions:

Cook Corn:
- If using fresh corn, grill or boil the corn until it's cooked. If using frozen corn, cook according to package instructions. If using canned corn, drain and rinse.

Prepare Salad Dressing:
- In a large bowl, mix together mayonnaise, sour cream, crumbled cotija cheese, chopped cilantro, chili powder, minced garlic, and chopped jalapeño (if using).

Combine Corn and Dressing:
- Add the cooked and drained corn to the bowl with the dressing.

Toss Gently:
- Gently toss the corn with the dressing until well coated.

Chill (Optional):
- Refrigerate the Mexican Street Corn Salad for about 15-30 minutes to allow the flavors to meld, or serve it immediately.

Serve:
- Serve the salad in individual bowls or as a side dish. Garnish with extra crumbled cotija cheese, a sprinkle of chili powder, and lime wedges on the side.

This Mexican Street Corn Salad is a perfect balance of creamy, tangy, and spicy flavors. It's a great side dish for grilled meats, tacos, or as a standalone snack. Enjoy!

Potato Salad

Ingredients:

For the Potatoes:

- 2 pounds (about 1 kg) potatoes (Yukon Gold or red potatoes work well), peeled and diced into bite-sized pieces
- Salt, for boiling

For the Salad:

- 1/2 cup mayonnaise
- 2 tablespoons Dijon mustard
- 1 tablespoon apple cider vinegar
- 1/2 cup celery, finely chopped
- 1/4 cup red onion, finely chopped
- 2 tablespoons fresh parsley, chopped
- Salt and black pepper, to taste
- Optional: Hard-boiled eggs, chopped chives, or crispy bacon for garnish

Instructions:

Cook Potatoes:
- Place the diced potatoes in a large pot of salted water. Bring to a boil and cook until the potatoes are fork-tender but not mushy. This usually takes about 10-15 minutes. Drain the potatoes and let them cool to room temperature.

Prepare Dressing:
- In a small bowl, whisk together mayonnaise, Dijon mustard, apple cider vinegar, salt, and black pepper.

Assemble the Salad:
- In a large mixing bowl, combine the cooled diced potatoes with the chopped celery, red onion, and fresh parsley.

Add Dressing:
- Pour the dressing over the potato mixture.

Gently Toss:
- Gently toss the Potato Salad until the potatoes are well coated with the dressing.

Chill (Optional):

- Refrigerate the Potato Salad for at least 1-2 hours before serving to allow the flavors to meld. This step is optional, and you can serve it immediately if preferred.

Garnish (Optional):
- Before serving, garnish the Potato Salad with chopped hard-boiled eggs, chives, or crispy bacon.

Serve:
- Serve the Potato Salad chilled or at room temperature as a side dish for various meals.

This Potato Salad is a classic crowd-pleaser, and you can customize it by adding your favorite ingredients like pickles, mustard seeds, or a hint of paprika. Enjoy!

Roasted Brussels Sprouts Salad

Ingredients:

For the Roasted Brussels Sprouts:

- 1 pound Brussels sprouts, trimmed and halved
- 2 tablespoons olive oil
- Salt and black pepper, to taste
- 1 teaspoon garlic powder (optional)

For the Salad:

- 4 cups mixed salad greens (arugula, spinach, or your favorite greens)
- 1/2 cup dried cranberries
- 1/2 cup chopped pecans or walnuts, toasted
- 1/4 cup crumbled feta cheese or goat cheese

For the Balsamic Vinaigrette:

- 3 tablespoons balsamic vinegar
- 2 tablespoons extra virgin olive oil
- 1 teaspoon Dijon mustard
- 1 teaspoon honey or maple syrup
- Salt and black pepper, to taste

Instructions:

Roast Brussels Sprouts:
- Preheat the oven to 400°F (200°C).
- Toss the halved Brussels sprouts with olive oil, salt, pepper, and garlic powder (if using).
- Spread them on a baking sheet in a single layer. Roast for 20-25 minutes or until the Brussels sprouts are golden brown and crispy on the edges. Stir halfway through cooking.

Prepare Salad Greens:
- In a large salad bowl, place the mixed salad greens.

Assemble the Salad:
- Add the roasted Brussels sprouts, dried cranberries, toasted chopped nuts, and crumbled feta cheese to the salad bowl.

Make the Balsamic Vinaigrette:
- In a small bowl, whisk together balsamic vinegar, extra virgin olive oil, Dijon mustard, honey or maple syrup, salt, and black pepper.

Drizzle Dressing:
- Drizzle the balsamic vinaigrette over the salad.

Toss Gently:
- Gently toss the Roasted Brussels Sprouts Salad until all ingredients are well coated with the dressing.

Serve:
- Serve the salad immediately as a flavorful and satisfying side dish or as a light meal on its own.

This Roasted Brussels Sprouts Salad is a perfect combination of textures and flavors, offering a delicious twist on a classic vegetable. Enjoy!

Italian Pasta Salad

Ingredients:

For the Salad:

- 8 ounces (about 225g) rotini or fusilli pasta, cooked and cooled
- 1 cup cherry tomatoes, halved
- 1 cup cucumber, diced
- 1/2 cup red bell pepper, diced
- 1/2 cup black olives, sliced
- 1/2 cup mozzarella cheese, cubed
- 1/4 cup red onion, finely chopped
- 1/4 cup fresh basil, chopped

For the Italian Dressing:

- 1/3 cup extra virgin olive oil
- 3 tablespoons red wine vinegar
- 1 teaspoon Dijon mustard
- 1 clove garlic, minced
- 1 teaspoon dried oregano
- 1 teaspoon dried basil
- Salt and black pepper, to taste

Instructions:

Cook Pasta:
- Cook the pasta according to package instructions. Once cooked, rinse under cold water to stop the cooking process and cool the pasta.

Prepare Vegetables:
- In a large salad bowl, combine the halved cherry tomatoes, diced cucumber, diced red bell pepper, sliced black olives, cubed mozzarella cheese, finely chopped red onion, and chopped fresh basil.

Assemble the Salad:
- Add the cooled pasta to the bowl with the vegetables.

Make the Italian Dressing:
- In a small bowl, whisk together extra virgin olive oil, red wine vinegar, Dijon mustard, minced garlic, dried oregano, dried basil, salt, and black pepper.

Drizzle Dressing:

- Drizzle the Italian dressing over the pasta and vegetable mixture.

Toss Gently:
- Gently toss the Italian Pasta Salad until all ingredients are well coated with the dressing.

Chill (Optional):
- Refrigerate the salad for about 30 minutes to let the flavors meld, or serve it immediately.

Serve:
- Serve the Italian Pasta Salad as a refreshing side dish or a light and satisfying meal.

This Italian Pasta Salad is perfect for picnics, potlucks, or as a side dish for grilled meats. It's versatile, customizable, and always a crowd-pleaser. Enjoy!

Tomato and Mozzarella Salad

Ingredients:

For the Salad:

- 4 large tomatoes, sliced
- 1 pound fresh mozzarella cheese, sliced
- Fresh basil leaves
- Extra virgin olive oil, for drizzling
- Balsamic glaze (optional)
- Salt and black pepper, to taste

Instructions:

Slice Tomatoes and Mozzarella:
- Wash and slice the tomatoes and fresh mozzarella into 1/4-inch thick slices.

Assemble the Salad:
- Arrange the tomato and mozzarella slices alternately on a serving platter or individual plates.

Add Basil:
- Place fresh basil leaves between the tomato and mozzarella slices.

Drizzle Olive Oil:
- Drizzle extra virgin olive oil over the Tomato and Mozzarella Salad.

Season:
- Sprinkle salt and black pepper to taste over the salad.

Optional Balsamic Glaze:
- Optionally, drizzle balsamic glaze over the salad for added flavor.

Serve:
- Serve the Tomato and Mozzarella Salad immediately as a light and refreshing appetizer or side dish.

This Caprese Salad is a delightful way to showcase the flavors of summer with its vibrant colors and simple, yet delicious, ingredients. Enjoy the classic combination of tomatoes, mozzarella, and basil!

Cucumber Dill Salad

Ingredients:

For the Salad:

- 3 medium cucumbers, thinly sliced
- 1/2 red onion, thinly sliced
- 2 tablespoons fresh dill, chopped
- Salt and black pepper, to taste

For the Dressing:

- 1/3 cup Greek yogurt or sour cream
- 2 tablespoons mayonnaise
- 1 tablespoon white vinegar
- 1 tablespoon fresh lemon juice
- 1 teaspoon sugar
- 1 clove garlic, minced (optional)
- Salt and black pepper, to taste

Instructions:

Prepare Cucumbers and Onion:
- Wash and thinly slice the cucumbers. Thinly slice the red onion.

Make the Dressing:
- In a small bowl, whisk together Greek yogurt or sour cream, mayonnaise, white vinegar, fresh lemon juice, sugar, minced garlic (if using), salt, and black pepper. Adjust the seasonings to taste.

Combine Ingredients:
- In a large salad bowl, combine the sliced cucumbers, sliced red onion, and chopped fresh dill.

Add Dressing:
- Pour the dressing over the cucumber mixture.

Toss Gently:
- Gently toss the Cucumber Dill Salad until the vegetables are well coated with the dressing.

Chill (Optional):
- Refrigerate the salad for about 15-30 minutes to allow the flavors to meld, or serve it immediately.

Serve:
- Serve the Cucumber Dill Salad as a refreshing side dish for summer gatherings or as a light and healthy snack.

This salad is a wonderful way to enjoy the crispness of cucumbers combined with the aromatic freshness of dill. It pairs well with grilled meats, fish, or as a simple side for any meal. Enjoy!

Caesar Pasta Salad

Ingredients:

For the Salad:

- 8 ounces (about 225g) penne or your favorite pasta, cooked and cooled
- 2 cups cooked and shredded chicken breast (optional)
- 1 cup cherry tomatoes, halved
- 1/2 cup black olives, sliced
- 1/2 cup grated Parmesan cheese
- 1/4 cup fresh parsley, chopped
- 1/4 cup croutons, roughly crushed

For the Caesar Dressing:

- 1/2 cup mayonnaise
- 1/4 cup grated Parmesan cheese
- 2 tablespoons lemon juice
- 1 tablespoon Dijon mustard
- 2 cloves garlic, minced
- 1 teaspoon Worcestershire sauce
- Salt and black pepper, to taste

Instructions:

Cook Pasta:
- Cook the pasta according to package instructions. Once cooked, rinse under cold water to stop the cooking process and cool the pasta.

Prepare Salad Ingredients:
- In a large bowl, combine the cooled pasta, shredded chicken (if using), cherry tomatoes, sliced black olives, grated Parmesan cheese, fresh parsley, and crushed croutons.

Make the Caesar Dressing:
- In a small bowl, whisk together mayonnaise, grated Parmesan cheese, lemon juice, Dijon mustard, minced garlic, Worcestershire sauce, salt, and black pepper.

Add Dressing:
- Pour the Caesar dressing over the pasta and other ingredients.

Toss Gently:

- Gently toss the Caesar Pasta Salad until everything is well coated with the dressing.

Chill (Optional):
- Refrigerate the salad for about 15-30 minutes to allow the flavors to meld, or serve it immediately.

Serve:
- Serve the Caesar Pasta Salad as a satisfying and flavorful main dish or as a side for your favorite grilled meats.

This Caesar Pasta Salad is a perfect choice for a quick and tasty meal, combining the classic Caesar flavors with the heartiness of pasta. Enjoy!

Chicken and Quinoa Salad

Ingredients:

For the Salad:

- 1 cup quinoa, rinsed and cooked according to package instructions
- 1 pound boneless, skinless chicken breasts, grilled and sliced
- 1 cup cherry tomatoes, halved
- 1 cucumber, diced
- 1 bell pepper (any color), diced
- 1/4 cup red onion, finely chopped
- 1/4 cup feta cheese, crumbled
- 1/4 cup Kalamata olives, sliced
- Fresh parsley or cilantro, chopped (for garnish)

For the Dressing:

- 3 tablespoons extra virgin olive oil
- 2 tablespoons red wine vinegar
- 1 teaspoon Dijon mustard
- 1 clove garlic, minced
- 1 teaspoon honey or maple syrup
- Salt and black pepper, to taste

Instructions:

Cook Quinoa:
- Rinse quinoa under cold water. Cook quinoa according to package instructions. Once cooked, let it cool to room temperature.

Grill Chicken:
- Season chicken breasts with salt and pepper. Grill until fully cooked, then slice into strips.

Prepare Vegetables:
- In a large bowl, combine the cooked and cooled quinoa with cherry tomatoes, diced cucumber, diced bell pepper, finely chopped red onion, crumbled feta cheese, and sliced Kalamata olives.

Add Grilled Chicken:
- Add the sliced grilled chicken to the bowl with the vegetables and quinoa.

Make the Dressing:

- In a small bowl, whisk together extra virgin olive oil, red wine vinegar, Dijon mustard, minced garlic, honey or maple syrup, salt, and black pepper.

Drizzle Dressing:
- Drizzle the dressing over the Chicken and Quinoa Salad.

Toss Gently:
- Gently toss the salad until all ingredients are well coated with the dressing.

Chill (Optional):
- Refrigerate the salad for about 15-30 minutes to let the flavors meld, or serve it immediately.

Garnish:
- Garnish the salad with chopped fresh parsley or cilantro before serving.

Serve:
- Serve the Chicken and Quinoa Salad as a nutritious and satisfying main dish or as a hearty side.

This Chicken and Quinoa Salad is not only delicious but also packed with protein, making it a well-balanced and healthy meal option. Enjoy!

Roasted Red Pepper and Artichoke Salad

Ingredients:

For the Salad:

- 2 large red bell peppers
- 1 can (14 ounces) artichoke hearts, drained and quartered
- 1/2 cup Kalamata olives, pitted and sliced
- 1/4 cup red onion, finely chopped
- 1/4 cup fresh parsley, chopped
- 1/4 cup feta cheese, crumbled (optional)
- Mixed salad greens (arugula, spinach, or your choice)

For the Dressing:

- 3 tablespoons extra virgin olive oil
- 1 tablespoon balsamic vinegar
- 1 clove garlic, minced
- 1 teaspoon Dijon mustard
- Salt and black pepper, to taste

Instructions:

Roast Red Peppers:
- Preheat the oven broiler. Place red bell peppers on a baking sheet and broil, turning occasionally, until the skin is charred and blistered. Transfer the peppers to a bowl, cover with plastic wrap, and let them steam for about 10 minutes. Peel off the skin, remove seeds, and slice the peppers into strips.

Prepare Artichokes:
- Drain and quarter the artichoke hearts.

Assemble the Salad:
- In a large salad bowl, combine the roasted red pepper strips, quartered artichoke hearts, sliced Kalamata olives, finely chopped red onion, chopped fresh parsley, and crumbled feta cheese (if using).

Make the Dressing:
- In a small bowl, whisk together extra virgin olive oil, balsamic vinegar, minced garlic, Dijon mustard, salt, and black pepper.

Drizzle Dressing:

- Drizzle the dressing over the salad.

Toss Gently:
- Gently toss the Roasted Red Pepper and Artichoke Salad until all ingredients are well coated with the dressing.

Serve on Greens:
- Serve the salad on a bed of mixed salad greens, such as arugula or spinach.

Garnish (Optional):
- Garnish with additional fresh parsley or crumbled feta cheese.

Serve:
- Serve the Roasted Red Pepper and Artichoke Salad as a flavorful and colorful side dish or a light meal.

This salad is not only delicious but also visually appealing, making it a great addition to any meal or gathering. Enjoy!

Spring Mix Salad with Raspberry Vinaigrette

Ingredients:

For the Salad:

- 4 cups spring mix lettuce (a combination of baby greens like arugula, spinach, and mixed lettuces)
- 1 cup cherry tomatoes, halved
- 1/2 cucumber, thinly sliced
- 1/4 cup red onion, thinly sliced
- 1/4 cup feta cheese, crumbled
- 1/4 cup candied pecans or walnuts (optional)

For the Raspberry Vinaigrette:

- 1/2 cup fresh raspberries
- 3 tablespoons extra virgin olive oil
- 2 tablespoons red wine vinegar
- 1 tablespoon honey or maple syrup
- 1 teaspoon Dijon mustard
- Salt and black pepper, to taste

Instructions:

Prepare Salad Greens:
- In a large salad bowl, combine the spring mix lettuce.

Add Vegetables:
- Add the halved cherry tomatoes, thinly sliced cucumber, thinly sliced red onion, crumbled feta cheese, and candied pecans or walnuts (if using).

Make Raspberry Vinaigrette:
- In a blender or food processor, combine fresh raspberries, extra virgin olive oil, red wine vinegar, honey or maple syrup, Dijon mustard, salt, and black pepper. Blend until smooth.

Strain (Optional):
- If you prefer a smoother dressing, you can strain the raspberry vinaigrette using a fine mesh sieve to remove the seeds.

Drizzle Dressing:
- Drizzle the raspberry vinaigrette over the spring mix salad.

Toss Gently:

- Gently toss the salad until all ingredients are well coated with the dressing.

Serve:
- Serve the Spring Mix Salad with Raspberry Vinaigrette as a refreshing and vibrant side dish.

Garnish (Optional):
- Garnish with additional fresh raspberries or a sprinkle of feta cheese.

This Spring Mix Salad with Raspberry Vinaigrette is a perfect choice for a light lunch or as a side dish for grilled chicken or fish. The sweet and tangy flavors of the dressing complement the fresh greens beautifully. Enjoy!

Edamame and Sesame Salad

Ingredients:

For the Salad:

- 2 cups cooked and shelled edamame (thawed if using frozen)
- 1 cup shredded red cabbage
- 1 carrot, julienned or grated
- 1 red bell pepper, thinly sliced
- 2 green onions, sliced
- 2 tablespoons sesame seeds (toasted for extra flavor)
- Fresh cilantro or parsley, chopped (for garnish)

For the Sesame Dressing:

- 3 tablespoons soy sauce
- 2 tablespoons rice vinegar
- 1 tablespoon sesame oil
- 1 tablespoon honey or maple syrup
- 1 clove garlic, minced
- 1 teaspoon grated fresh ginger
- 1 tablespoon neutral oil (vegetable or canola)
- Black pepper, to taste

Instructions:

Prepare Edamame:
- If using frozen edamame, cook according to package instructions. If using fresh, boil or steam until tender, then shell.

Prepare Vegetables:
- In a large bowl, combine the cooked and shelled edamame with shredded red cabbage, julienned or grated carrot, thinly sliced red bell pepper, sliced green onions, and toasted sesame seeds.

Make Sesame Dressing:
- In a small bowl, whisk together soy sauce, rice vinegar, sesame oil, honey or maple syrup, minced garlic, grated fresh ginger, neutral oil, and black pepper.

Drizzle Dressing:
- Drizzle the sesame dressing over the edamame and vegetable mixture.

Toss Gently:
- Gently toss the Edamame and Sesame Salad until all ingredients are well coated with the dressing.

Chill (Optional):
- Refrigerate the salad for about 15-30 minutes to allow the flavors to meld, or serve it immediately.

Garnish:
- Garnish the salad with chopped fresh cilantro or parsley before serving.

Serve:
- Serve the Edamame and Sesame Salad as a flavorful and nutrient-packed side dish or a light and satisfying meal.

This salad is not only delicious but also rich in protein and fiber, making it a healthy addition to your menu. Enjoy the combination of vibrant colors and flavors!

Caprese Pasta Salad

Ingredients:

For the Salad:

- 8 ounces (about 225g) rotini or your favorite pasta, cooked and cooled
- 1 pint cherry tomatoes, halved
- 8 ounces fresh mozzarella balls (ciliegine), halved
- 1/2 cup fresh basil leaves, torn
- Salt and black pepper, to taste

For the Balsamic Vinaigrette:

- 1/4 cup extra virgin olive oil
- 2 tablespoons balsamic vinegar
- 1 teaspoon Dijon mustard
- 1 clove garlic, minced
- Salt and black pepper, to taste

Instructions:

Cook Pasta:
- Cook the pasta according to package instructions. Once cooked, rinse under cold water to stop the cooking process and cool the pasta.

Prepare Salad Ingredients:
- In a large salad bowl, combine the cooled pasta with halved cherry tomatoes, halved fresh mozzarella balls, and torn fresh basil leaves.

Make Balsamic Vinaigrette:
- In a small bowl, whisk together extra virgin olive oil, balsamic vinegar, Dijon mustard, minced garlic, salt, and black pepper.

Drizzle Dressing:
- Drizzle the balsamic vinaigrette over the pasta and other ingredients.

Toss Gently:
- Gently toss the Caprese Pasta Salad until everything is well coated with the dressing.

Chill (Optional):
- Refrigerate the salad for about 15-30 minutes to let the flavors meld, or serve it immediately.

Serve:

- Serve the Caprese Pasta Salad as a refreshing and satisfying side dish or a light meal.

Garnish (Optional):
- Garnish with additional fresh basil leaves and a drizzle of balsamic glaze.

This Caprese Pasta Salad is perfect for summer picnics, potlucks, or as a side dish for grilled proteins. The combination of pasta with the classic Caprese ingredients makes it a crowd-pleaser. Enjoy!

Orange and Almond Salad

Ingredients:

For the Salad:

- 4 large oranges, peeled and segmented
- 1/2 cup sliced almonds, toasted
- Mixed salad greens (arugula, spinach, or your choice)
- 1/4 cup red onion, thinly sliced
- Fresh mint leaves, for garnish

For the Citrus Vinaigrette:

- 3 tablespoons extra virgin olive oil
- 2 tablespoons orange juice
- 1 tablespoon lemon juice
- 1 teaspoon honey or maple syrup
- 1 teaspoon Dijon mustard
- Salt and black pepper, to taste

Instructions:

Prepare Oranges:
- Peel the oranges and separate them into segments. Remove any seeds.

Toast Almonds:
- In a dry skillet over medium heat, toast the sliced almonds until they are golden brown and fragrant. Stir frequently to prevent burning.

Assemble the Salad:
- In a large salad bowl, combine the orange segments with the mixed salad greens, toasted sliced almonds, and thinly sliced red onion.

Make the Citrus Vinaigrette:
- In a small bowl, whisk together extra virgin olive oil, orange juice, lemon juice, honey or maple syrup, Dijon mustard, salt, and black pepper.

Drizzle Dressing:
- Drizzle the citrus vinaigrette over the salad.

Toss Gently:
- Gently toss the Orange and Almond Salad until all ingredients are well coated with the dressing.

Chill (Optional):

- Refrigerate the salad for about 15-30 minutes to allow the flavors to meld, or serve it immediately.

Garnish:
- Garnish the salad with fresh mint leaves before serving.

Serve:
- Serve the Orange and Almond Salad as a light and refreshing side dish or a healthy and satisfying meal.

This salad is not only visually appealing but also a great way to enjoy the natural sweetness of oranges combined with the crunch of almonds. It's perfect for a light lunch or as a side for various main courses. Enjoy!